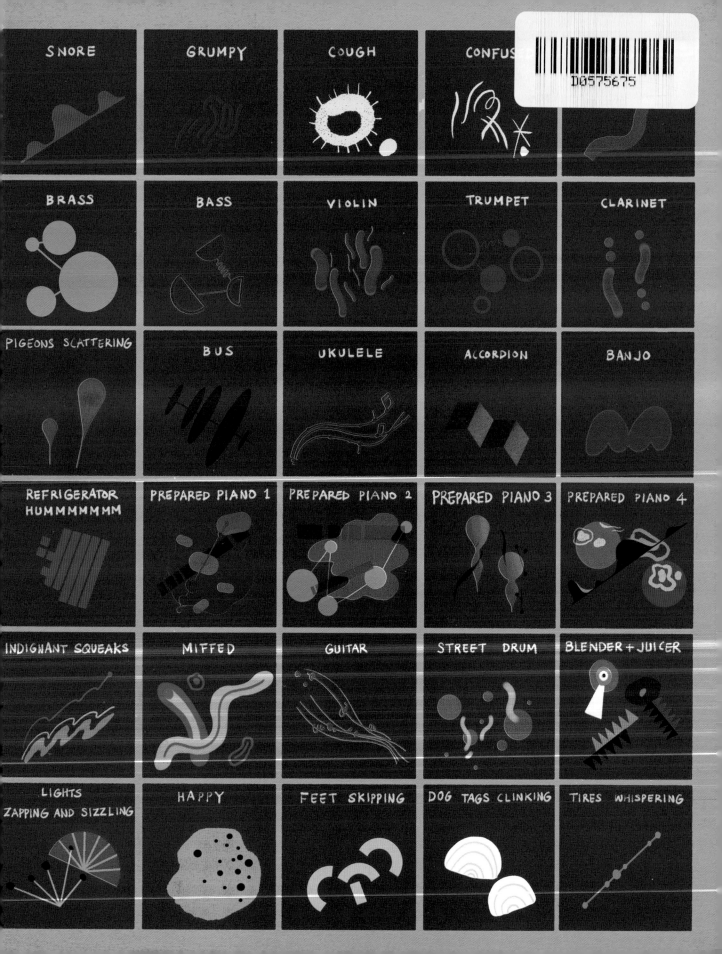

TO NINA SCHWARTZ KAHN, WHO ALWAYS LISTENS,
AND IN MEMORY OF COMPOSER ELLIOTT SCHWARTZ,
WHO EMBRACED THE IDEA OF THIS PROJECT. —L.R.

FOR THE ONES WHO HAVE CURIOUS EARS. —I.S.N.

The author wishes to thank Laura Kuhn,
trustee and executive director of the John Cage Trust,
and composer Peter Dickinson
for their encouragement and assistance.

Text copyright © 2023 by Lisa Jean Rogers
Jacket art and interior illustrations copyright © 2023 by Il Sung Na.

All rights reserved. Published in the United States by Anne Schwartz Books, an imprint of Random House
Children's Books, a division of Penguin Random House LLC, New York.

Anne Schwartz Books and the colophon are trademarks of Penguin Random House LLC.

Visit us on the Web! rhcbooks.com
Educators and librarians, for a variety of teaching tools, visit us at RHTeachersLibrarians.com

Library of Congress Cataloging-in-Publication Data
Names: Rogers, Lisa Jean, author. | Na, Il Sung, illustrator.
Title: Beautiful noise: the music of John Cage / Lisa J. Rogers; [illustrations] Il Sung Na.
Description: First edition. | New York: Anne Schwartz Books, 2023. | Includes bibliographical references. |
Audience: Ages 4–8 | Audience: Grades K–1 | Summary: "A picture book biography about pioneering composer,
John Cage"—Provided by publisher.
Identifiers: LCCN 2022048833 | ISBN 978-0-593-64662-5 (hardcover) | ISBN 978-0-593-64663-2 (lib. bdg.) |
ISBN 978-0-593-64664-9 (ebook)
Subjects: LCSH: Cage, John—Juvenile literature. | Composers—United States—Biography—Juvenile literature. |
Avant-garde (Music)—United States—Juvenile literature.
Classification: LCC ML3930.C18 R64 2023 | DDC 780.92 [B]—dc23/eng/20221011

The text of this book is set in 14-point Meta Pro.
The illustrations were rendered in Adobe Fresco.
Book design by Sarah Hokanson.

MANUFACTURED IN CHINA
10 9 8 7 6 5 4 3 2 1   First Edition

BEAUTIFUL NOISE

THE MUSIC OF JOHN CAGE

By Lisa Rogers

Illustrated by Il Sung Na

a·s·b

anne schwartz books

I CAN'T UNDERSTAND WHY PEOPLE ARE FRIGHTENED OF NEW IDEAS.
I'M FRIGHTENED OF THE OLD ONES.
—JOHN CAGE

What if . . .

all the sounds you heard . . .

a garbage truck screeching

feet skipping

pigeons scattering

tires whispering

cats hissing

children giggling

balls bouncing

dog tags clinking

taxis vrooming . . .

sounded to you like music?

Then you'd be like John Cage.

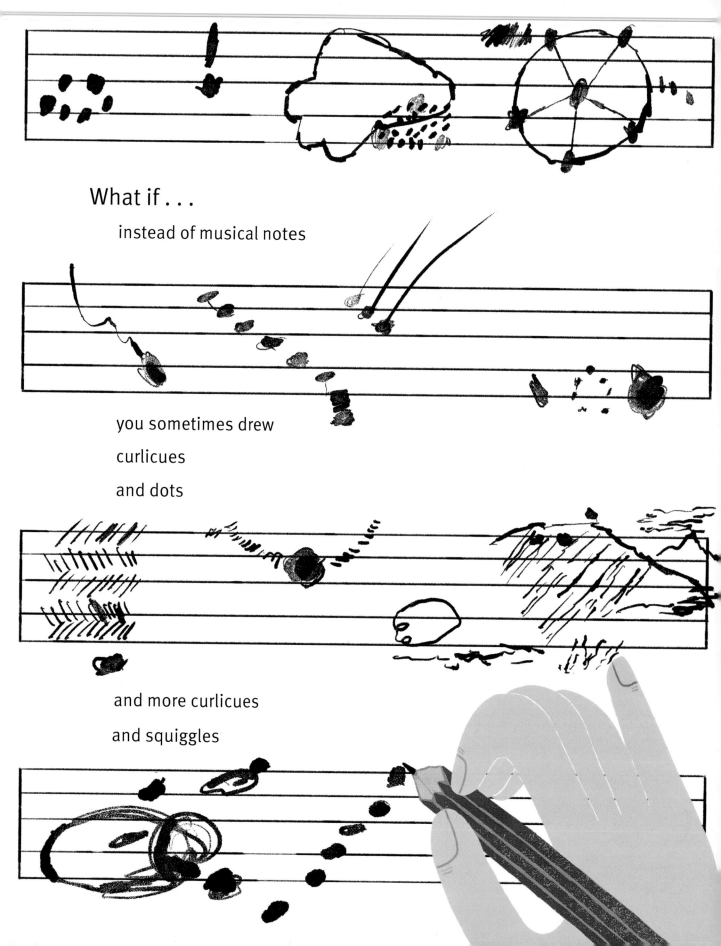

What if . . .

instead of musical notes

you sometimes drew

curlicues

and dots

and more curlicues

and squiggles

and asked musicians to play them like notes
however they wanted
with whatever instruments they wanted
and they did?

Then you'd be like John Cage.

What if you wished a piano

could sound like a whole orchestra

so you stuck erasers and bolts and screws

between and under its strings

and made music no one had ever heard before?

Then you'd be like John Cage.

What if you composed a piece of piano music
without any notes
and invited people to a barn to hear it
and . . .

for exactly

four minutes

were the sound of the wind

and rain

and people grumbling

that they didn't hear music

but you did?

Then you'd be like John Cage.

What if you held another concert

    and when the harpist plucked her harp

    and the timpanist struck his drums

    and the horn players blew their horns

and the violinists bowed their violins

and, well, all the musicians

really *did* play their instruments . . .

you turned their microphones

on and off and

Then you'd be like John Cage.

What if people stormed out of these concerts
and said your music wasn't music

but you still believed
it was?

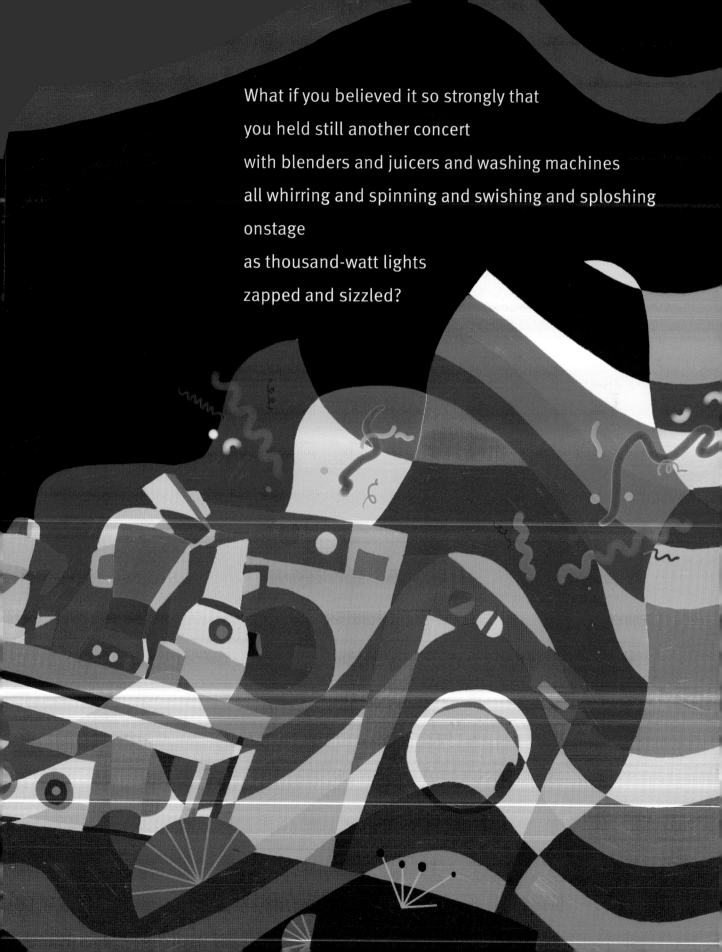

What if you believed it so strongly that

you held still another concert

with blenders and juicers and washing machines

all whirring and spinning and swishing and sploshing

onstage

as thousand-watt lights

zapped and sizzled?

And what if you concentrated so hard

during that concert

that you didn't notice

whether people were laughing or clapping

or even if your pants were catching on fire

but you did notice the sound

of this new music?

What if you knew

    that this music was unique,

    that this music was important,

    and that *any* noise could be beautiful?

    And you knew that loving all sounds—

except the refrigerator's hummmmm
but you were trying to love that too—
and sharing them
made the world more joyful?
Then you'd be like John Cage.

Yet . . .

you don't have to
bang on a bathtub
or
brush cactus spines with a feather
or
blow a seashell like a trumpet
or do any of the things he did,
except for one.
To be like John Cage,
the only thing
you have to do . . .

is listen.

"If you asked me what music I like most," John Cage said, "I'd reply: 'The sounds around me, the sounds that I haven't composed.'"

For John Cage (1912–1992), any sound could be music, music was everywhere, and there was no such thing as silence. The son of an inventor, he spent his life experimenting with ways to combine ordinary sounds (like people laughing, horns beeping, and sirens wailing) to invent new sounds for the music he composed. Influenced by Zen philosophy, he believed that if people could enjoy sounds they thought of as noise, they would be happier.

Many people didn't understand Cage's work, but his fearless dedication to experimentation was groundbreaking. He is considered one of the most influential composers of the twentieth century.

There was always something new to experience at a John Cage concert, and even the composer didn't know exactly what the music would sound like. For some performances, he'd tune radios to different stations; whatever sounds were aired became the music. He tossed coins and consulted the I Ching, an ancient Chinese text, allowing chance to decide a sound's type, length, and loudness. For some pieces, he specified that conductors could choose how much of it to perform and the type and number of instruments.

Cage stuck objects on and between piano strings to create an orchestra's worth of sound in a single instrument. He created a kind of theater with *Water Walk* (1959), in which he let steam escape from a pressure cooker, blew a duck whistle, and crushed ice cubes in a blender. For *Fontana Mix* (1958), he specified that his squiggle-like drawings of notes could be interpreted in any way the performer chose.

He pioneered electronic music. For *Williams Mix* (1952), he used about 600 sounds recorded on magnetic tape, the predecessor of digital recording. He spent a year slicing, arranging, and reattaching bits of tape, even specifying the angle for cutting each tiny segment. The four-minute musical piece used eight tape machines to play back the 3,000 spliced bits of tape.

Atlas Eclipticalis, composed to be performed with his partner Merce Cunningham's dance *Aeon*, caused the audience and New York Philharmonic musicians to walk out of a 1964 concert. Cage arranged his notes according to a map of the stars. He laid transparent paper printed with a musical staff over the star map. Then he marked the positions of the stars on the staff, which became the notes of the composition.

Cage found joy in his process and its results, however unexpected. His pants really did begin to smolder from the lamps' intense heat during his 1966 performance of *Variations VII*. "Isn't that marvelous?" Cage remarked.

Cage's "silent" piece, *4' 33"*, premiered in 1952 in Woodstock, New York, with the pianist closing and opening the keyboard lid to represent each movement. The only sounds were unplanned—a bit of rain pattering the metal roof, a swish of wind outside, and an audience complaining that Cage's music was a ridiculous joke.

He wasn't joking. He was serious about asking people to accept new ideas, recognize music in everyday life, and be still enough to hear sounds in silence.

Children would understand how to find music, Cage thought. "Let them write their own," he said. "The class takes a walk—listens to sounds—looks at rubbish to make sounds. A musical walk!"

AUTHOR'S SOURCES

"I can't understand why people are frightened . . .": Smith, 221.

"If you asked me . . .": Terkel.

"Isn't that marvelous?": Cage, John, et al. *Variations VII*.

"Let them write their own . . .": John Cage conversation with Peter Dickinson.

ILLUSTRATOR'S NOTE

Who was John Cage? That's what I wondered when I first read Lisa Rogers's manuscript. Although I often listen to classical music, I had no idea. (I probably shouldn't admit this!) To find out more, I did a "John Cage" search on Google. I listened to John Cage music on YouTube. I read his inspirational book *Every Day Is a Good Day: The Visual Art of John Cage,* which was kindly sent to me by my editor. And I read and watched many interviews with Cage on different platforms. My research only made me more curious about this extraordinary person.

By now I knew I wanted to illustrate the book . . . but *how?* How could I make sound, something that isn't visual, visual? I needed to find an approach that was different from my other books and was excited when I hit upon the idea of using shapes and colors to represent each sound.

I was also captivated by the idea that silence can be music, and amazed at how Cage used sounds made by household objects. All of it opened my mind to the importance of *listening*—of paying attention to every sound around me—and informed my illustrations. And it made me rethink what music is.

Though almost everything I've drawn in these pages is factually accurate, I did take creative license in a few places, to help with visual flow and story. Cage lived on Eighteenth Street and Sixth Avenue in New York City, where he probably couldn't see Union Square from his window, but I placed his apartment overlooking the park. I also moved the piano and some windows into his kitchen and removed the door.

John Cage preparing a piano with bolts and screws in 1947.

I think it was an advantage that I began this process without knowing John Cage. There are still a lot of things I hope to learn about his mind, his music, and his deep creativity. But one thing I have already learned—and that I hope children will take away from this book—is that EVERYTHING IS MUSIC.

SELECTED SOURCES

Cage, John. Conversation with Peter Dickinson, shared with the author via email, October 14, 2016.

Cage, John, et al. *Variations VII.* New York: E.A.T. and ARTPIX. Distributed by Microcinema International, 2008. DVD.

johncage.org: website of the John Cage Trust

Smith, Arnold Jay. "Reaching for the Cosmos: A Composers' Colloquium," *Down Beat,* October 10, 1977, in Kostelanetz, Richard. *Conversing with Cage.* 2nd edition. New York: Routledge, 2003, 221.

Terkel, Studs. *Voices of Our Time: The Original Live Interviews.* Minneapolis: HighBridge Audio, 2005. DVD.

Tomkins, Calvin. "Figure in an Imaginary Landscape." *The New Yorker,* Nov. 28, 1964, 64–128.

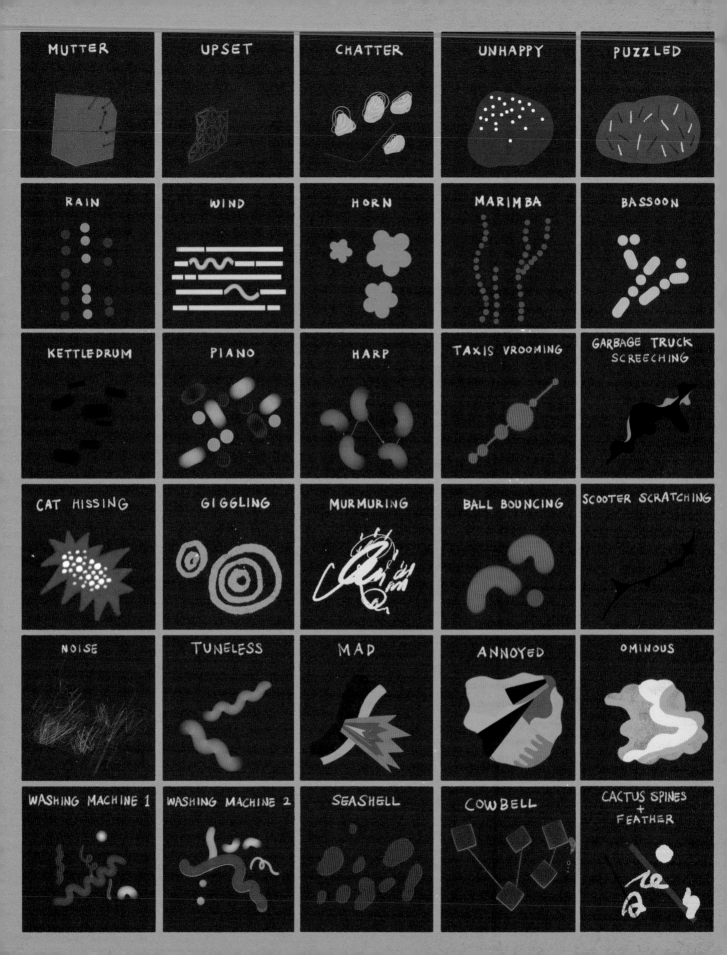